First Steps to
MASSAGE

Vera Harvey

AXIOM

ISBN: 1 86476 030 3

Axiom
Australia

Welcome

are the hands that with knead and stroke restore radiance to a body dull and tight.

Contents
page

Setting the Scene

This book is not intended to be a full course in massage, rather it has been designed to provide sufficient information to allow readers to give friends and family members a safe and revitalising massage in the comfort of their own homes.

You, as the massage giver, want the receiver to enjoy and benefit from the experience. To this end it is important that you prepare the massage area prior to its commencement. A relaxing massage is defeated if surroundings reflect anything other than peace and restful tranquillity.

Initially you will arrange a time for the massage where both you and the receiver know you don't have to hurry away to keep any appointments. Location, of course, is equally important, as a quiet spot where you will not be disturbed can only assist in the relaxation process.

Some soft relaxation music will add to the atmosphere, however ensure the receiver will enjoy music being played - some people prefer a quieter atmosphere. Lighting in most rooms tends to be harsh and intrusive - using small lamps or upward lighting is ideal as they create a soft intimate glow. Remove the telephone handpiece and ensure mobile phones are turned off - if a phone rings when a person is in deep relaxation they can easily be distracted.

Ideally, the receiver should lie on a padded massage table, (fig 1) placed in the centre of the room to allow you space without obstructing your movements. However, if such a table is not available alternatives can readily be found. You may use a firm bed; a floor could be suitable, or simply a chair or stool. It is important to recognise both you and the receiver must feel comfortable and at ease.

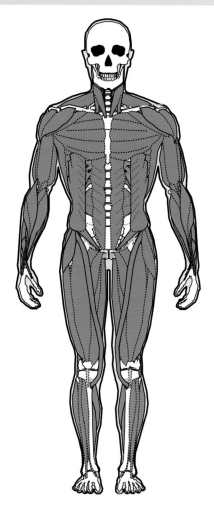

Muscles, superficial layer, front view
The human body contains more than 650 muscles, which
account for almost half the entire body weight.

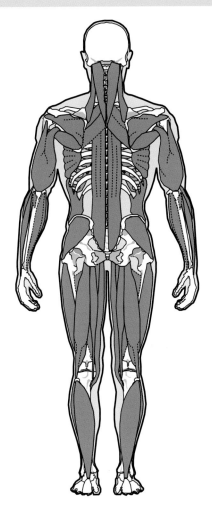

Muscles, deep layer, back view
Most muscles connect one bone with another and work by
pulling the bone as we move.

Setting the Scene

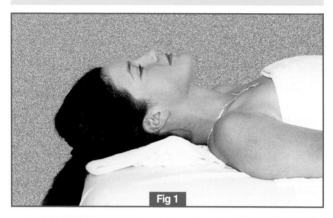

Fig 1

Make sure your room is warm. Warmth encourages relaxation.

Twenty-five degrees celsius is a good room temperature, as it will encourage the receiver's relaxation. Have a blanket, rug or extra towel nearby to place over the receiver. Check occasionally, ensuring the exposed limbs are warm enough, - cool air, even in summer can cause a chill during massage. Someone applying a massage may be feeling quite hot, but it is important to look after the comfort and well-being of the receiver, for health and possibly reasons of embarrassment. Some massage practitioners use head bands to avoid excess perspiration. As stated earlier best results will be achieved if the receiver is relaxed.

Occasional comments are fine, but having a full conversation is disruptive as the receiver's mind will become active. Tune into their breathing and only speak when necessary. Remember the objective of a massage is to treat the whole person; mind, body and emotions. The mind needs to retain a peaceful state of contentment.

To Help With The Massage

• Oils.

Cold pressed almond oil or apricot kernel oil are suitable for most skins, having the advantage of being good carrier oils if you choose to do an aromatherapy massage (more on aromatherapy is mentioned at the back of this book).

• Two large bath towels.

These will maintain body warmth as body temperature drops while the receiver relaxes. Draping also gives a sense of security. Many people feel vulnerable when they remove their clothes. Helping the receivers sense of security allows them to decide which part of the body they would like massaged, and which clothing they wish not removed.

• A comfortable place to lie or sit.

A massage table is ideal if you have one available (fig 2), however a comfortable mat on the floor, a table or bed are as effective. Massages focusing on hands, feet, neck, shoulders, arms and legs, can be done with the receiver sitting in a comfortable chair. When seated with support for posture the back should be massaged to correct any tightness.

Helpful Hints

Ask the receiver if they have a sensitive skin, some people react to some oils, creams or lotions. This is not a contra indication but a precaution. When massaging a person with acne, it is inadvisable to give an oil massage in the affected areas, only massage the rest of the body with oils.

How Long Should A Massage Take

It is not essential for the recipient to receive a full body massage to obtain benefit. Body parts can be massaged independently and the receiver will achieve relaxation. In the following examples suggested time is stated to help give each body part the right amount of attention.

The person giving the massage should beforehand establish the time the session will take and stay with this timetable, helping both recipient and giver to maintain a sense of purpose and relaxation.

A full massage should take no longer than an hour and 20 minutes. Even though a massage is enjoyable, receivers tend to become restless after this period of time.

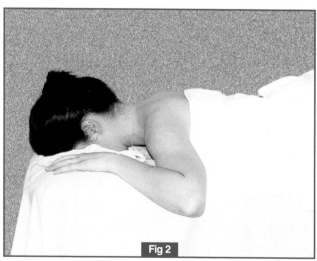

Fig 2

Make sure the receiver is as comfortable as possible.

Massage Sequences

This book uses some words you may not be familiar with:

Effleurage is the simplest massage technique. It makes use of long, flowing strokes either with a flat or cupped hand. It warms each body part before using more pressure on specific points. Effleurage is a French word meaning 'stroking' (fig 3).

Kneading is a well known massage technique which uses movements similar to those used to knead dough. The slower and deeper the strokes, the more beneficial kneading will be (fig 4).

Draining is a technique using your thumbpads to improve circulation whilst draining the body of toxins.

Friction is making small circular strokes with the fingers. It works through pressure and rotation to get deep into the muscles and nerve endings.

Feathering is a technique used to soothe the area you have been massaging. It leaves the receiver relaxed and feeling calm. Using the tips of your fingers you stroke lightly in a downward movement.

Butterfly is a motion of effleurage which covers a large area. Using both hands, start in the centre and move up the area then out to form 'butterfly wings' on the skin.

Massage

Caution

There may be occasions when it is unwise to massage. It is best to avoid massaging if the receiver has any of the following conditions:
- Fever or temperature
- Open wound
- Skin Infection
- Cancer
- Heart condition or high blood pressure
- Nausea
- Any abdominal pain
- Post-operative recovery
- Vascular surgery
- Severe back pain

Do not apply pressure on varicose veins

Do not massage directly on the spine. Work only on either side of the spinal column

If the receiver is pregnant, position her on her side during back and leg massages. Keep a number of pillows on hand in case the receiver requires extra support.

If you have any doubts it is advisable to check with a qualified medical practitioner before commencing the massage.

After kneading comes the draining process. Place your thumbpads side by side and push against the flow of the circulatory system (fig 5). In other words, push from the hand towards the top of the arm - or from the foot to the top of the leg. By draining towards the heart you will enhance the circulatory flow and enable toxins to leave the body via the urinary system. Draining also stimulates the lymphatic system, ridding it of waste products.

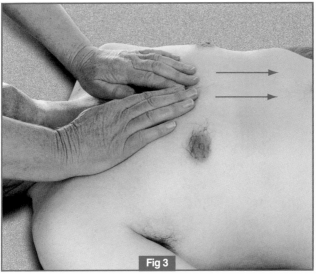

Fig 3

The correct effleurage hand positions.

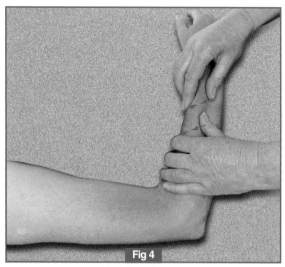

Kneading a forearm.

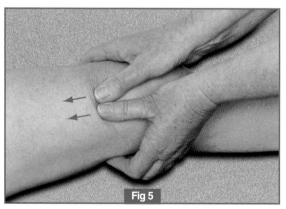

Correct position for draining.

When finished draining, use small, circular friction strokes to help relieve deep seated tension in both muscles and nerve endings (fig 6).

Finishing your massage, effleurage again and then feather the area. To feather, use the tips of your fingers and stroke lightly in a downward movement.

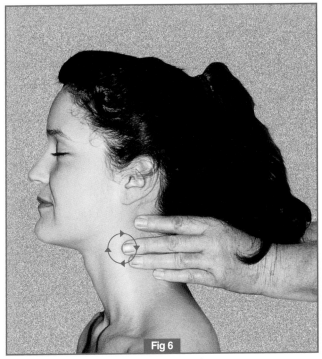

Fig 6

Friction strokes are great in neck massages.

Starting The Massage

The following pages help guide you through a full body massage, starting with the head and face and finishing with the back. The massage techniques you will be able to tailor to suit the receiver's individual needs. Remember to keep the massage under an hour and 20 minutes encouraging a restful massage. The time to be devoted to each body part are stated, helping you stay within this time limit. Of course these techniques and times will also help you devise area-specific massages so the receiver gets the maximum benefit.

To complete a full body massage you will normally need 25 to 30 mls of massage oil, however have more on hand in case the oil is absorbed quicker than anticipated. Extra oil may be necessary if the receiver has a large build or excessive body hair. **Be aware** that too much oil will stop you connecting with the receiver's skin, **too little** and your hands will cause friction and leave the receiver's skin sore.

Warming the oil helps relaxation. You can place the oil over a small ceramic oil burner to keep it warm - but be careful not to overheat it. If you do not have a burner, rub oil into your own hands before application.

Head

After a gentle effleurage, friction all over the scalp using fingers and thumbs in slow circular movements for 2 minutes. This relieves and relaxes, calms and soothes. The scalp holds more tension than most people realise!

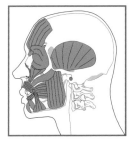

Face

Before beginning the massage, cleanse the face with a good facial cleanser removing any makeup and other toxins. Some ideal alternative cleansers are rose floral water, if the receiver is not wearing makeup, cedarwood floral water or peppermint floral water. Peppermint and cedarwood are especially good for cleansing male faces.

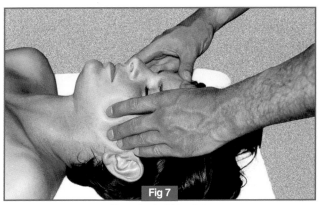

Fig 7

Removing facial tension.

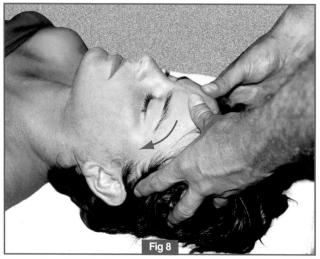

Fig 8

Friction applied to the forehead.

Face cleansing also assists with the relaxation process. If the receiver has acne or other skin problems do not massage the area with oils as they can aggravate the complaints. Use a light compression with your fingers and thumbs instead (fig 7).

Apply limited oil with your fingers to chin and forehead. Massage into the skin using your finger and thumb pads in small circular movements. Move your fingers slowly and rhythmically for approximately 2 minutes. Always use your finger and thumb pads as it is more comfortable for the receiver. By working from the centre of the face toward the temple and ears you will release excess pressure from the forehead and face (fig 8).

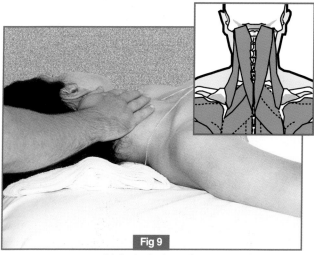

Fig 9

Friction in circular motions.

Avoid massaging on people with neck injuries or on the elderly as the neck is one of the most fragile areas of the body. When working on the neck, move the receiver's head slowly and gently. Do not apply pressure to the area over the carotid artery. This artery is on either side of the neck (fig 9).

When lifting the head, make sure receiver is still comfortable before starting the massage.

Effleurage on both sides of the neck, lifting the receiver's head slightly (fig 10), and pulling away from their shoulders using alternate hands. When using both your hands, turn the head to one side, letting it rest on one hand. Using the other hand, effleurage, and lightly squeeze the muscles between your fingers and thumbs. Turn the head to the other side and repeat the process. You should use 4 minutes to complete these steps.

From the sides of the neck effleurage both shoulders with flat hands in a circular sweeping motion around the front of the receiver's shoulders and up the back of the neck. You can be firmer when kneading the shoulders - using both hands work away from the neck across the top of the shoulders using fingers and thumbs.

If preferred this can be performed with the receiver in a sitting position (fig 11).

Butterfly effleurage, then integrate kneading into the neck and shoulders. Knead in this fashion 3 times. Finally finish off with gentle butterfly effleurage and feathering.

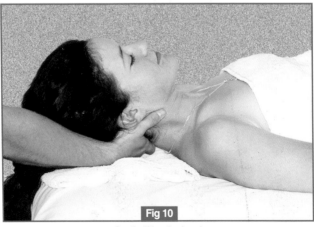

Fig 10

Gently lifting the head.

The way to health

is to have an aromatic bath and scented massage every day.

– Hippocrates

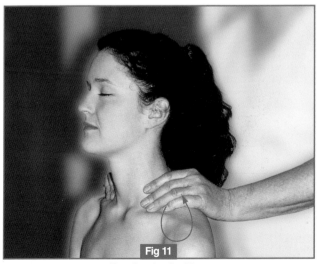

Fig 11

Kneading the shoulders.

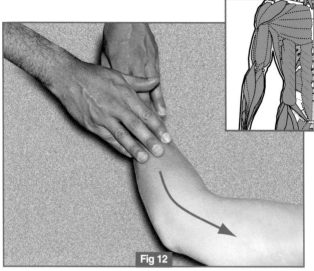

Fig 12

Effleuraging the arm with long flowing strokes.

Arms and hands are good parts of the body to massage for
the elderly as these areas are non-invasive, yet the massage
is still soothing.

Each arm should take 3 minutes to massage effectively.
Effleurage one arm with a flat hand using long strokes from
the wrist to the shoulder (fig 12). When effleuraging an arm,
repeat the movements 4 to 5 times ensuring muscle tissue is
properly warmed. Use oil as needed - skin on the arms often
absorbs oil very quickly. After warming the arm, knead from
wrist to shoulder, then back to the wrist. Knead the inside of
the arm 2 to 3 times and repeat on the outside of the arm (fig
13). Then turn the arm with the palm of the hand facing up.

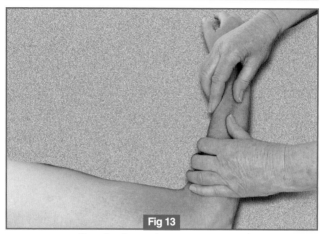

Fig 13

Kneading the arm from wrist to shoulder.

Drain from the wrist to the elbow and then across the forearm.
Place the receiver's arm back in a relaxed position -
effleurage and feather the area.

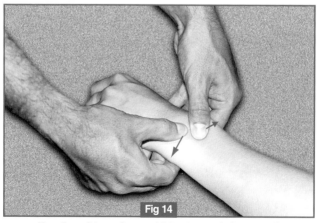

Fig 14

Kneading wrists can improve joint movement (refer page 24)

Hands

Hands and wrists are often forgotten. Massage them after each of the arms. Then knead both the inside and top of the wrist 2 to 3 times using your thumbs, moving from centre to the sides (fig 14). The hand requires very little oil.

First, stretch the back of the hand using the balls of your thumbs. Start in the centre of the hand and stretch to the sides and down the wrist (fig 15).

Then turn the hand palm up, making friction movements with your thumbs over the palm (fig 16). Turn the hand palm down and stretch the back of the hand once more.

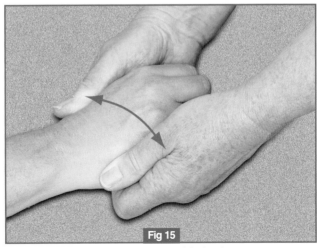

Fig 15

Stretching the back of the hand.

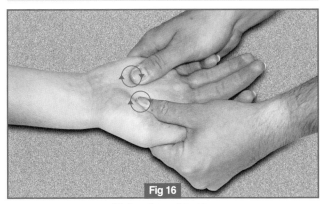

Friction all over the palm.

Fingers also need attention, particularly when the receiver suffers from stiff or sore joints. Gently stretch and knead each finger from the knuckle to the tip (fig 17).

Stretch the fingers again, effleurage and feather to finish the hand massage.

Each hand should take about 2 minutes.

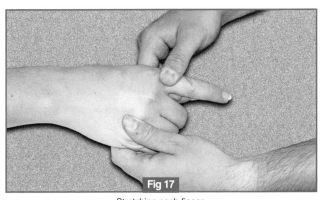

Stretching each finger.

Chest and Abdominals

As the chest and abdomen are considered private areas, make certain massaging these areas is acceptable. At all times be conscious of the receiver's body retaining its warmth. When the 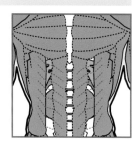 chest and abdomen are finished, re-drape the receiver, to retain both warmth and a sense of security.

Using a liberal amount of oil, warm the chest and torso by effleuraging in circular motions over the chest (fig 18) and

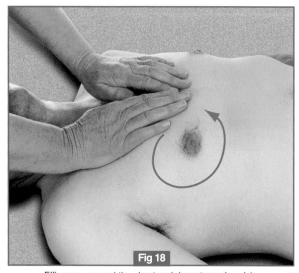

Fig 18

Effleurage around the chest and down towards pelvis.

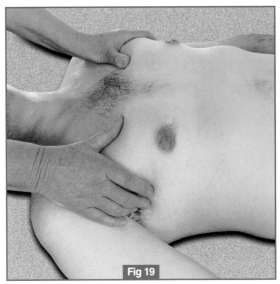

Fig 19

A deeper effleurage can be performed on male chests.

sweeping toward the pelvis. Massage more vigorously with deeper motions on the upper chest of a male (fig 19). Tension may collect in the area around the breastbone. Slow, gentle friction movements along the centre may be more helpful (fig 20).

Helpful Hints

Ask the receiver to give you feedback on the amount of pressure being applied. The massage should not induce pain or discomfort, it should be an enjoyable experience.

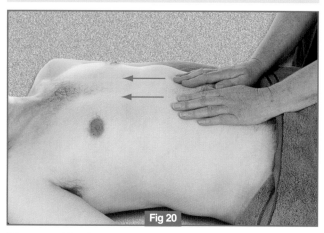

Fig 20

Then stand by the receiver's pelvis to butterfly effleurage their stomach and chest. Then effleurage the stomach, making circles on their abdomen using both hands and in a

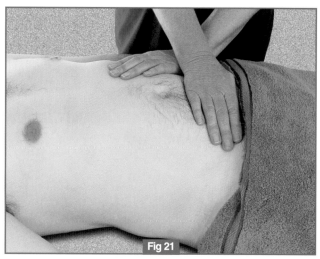

Fig 21

Effleurage of the stomach.

28

clockwise direction (fig 21). This technique moves in the same direction as the large colon (large intestine) and will help constipation sufferers. After circling, knead the abdomen to release tension (fig 22) and then circle once more. Repeat each step 4 to 5 times. Finish with effleurage and feathering. Allow 5 minutes to complete all movements.

Helpful Hints

It is a good idea to have the receiver take a few slow, deep breaths to induce relaxation just prior to the massage session.

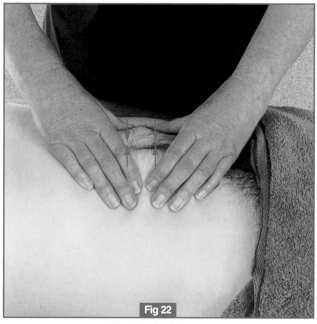

Fig 22

Kneading the abdomen.

Front Of Legs

Massaging the front of the legs is very similar to the way you massage arms. Using ample oil effleurage the entire leg from the ankle to the top of the thigh (fig 23). At this time a small amount of oil on the feet will make ready for a foot massage. Use 5 to 6 effleurage strokes on the legs using both hands.

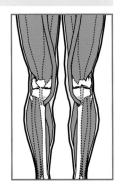

• After effleurage, knead the entire leg (fig 24). Being careful not to knock or jar the receiver's kneecap as this can be sensitive.

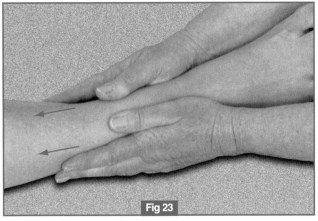

Fig 23

Effleurage on the legs

Helpful Hints

No body part needs more than 6 effleurage strokes to warm up.

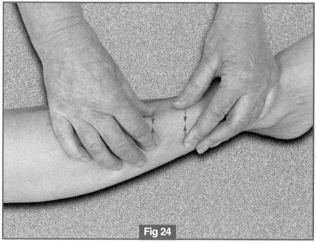

Kneading the lower leg.

- Then knead the inside and outside of the lower leg, repeating this 3 to 4 times.
- You only need to drain the top of the legs at the front (fig 25), but repeat the draining twice.

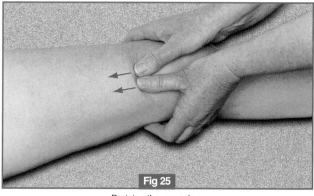

Draining the upper leg.

Massage

- Massage the leg again using butterfly effleurage as you come on to the thigh and reduce pressure as you return to the ankle.
- After doing this 3 to 4 times, feather from top to the foot to finish the front of the leg (fig 26).

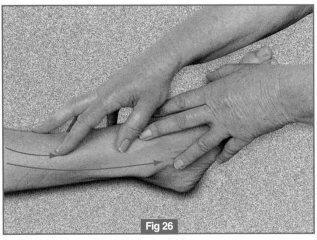

Fig 26

Feathering the leg.

be performed three to six times; any more may cause irritation to the area being massaged.

Reasonable pressure needs to be applied to the foot so use oil sparingly. Excessive oil is not easily absorbed and difficult to remove. The receiver might also slip after the massage is finished.

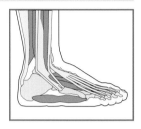

Sorbolene cream is a good alternative to oil in this instance.

Stretch the foot with your fingers and thumbs using sideways motions (fig 27). Each toe should then be stretched from the knuckle to the tip in the same way you stretched the fingers (fig 28).

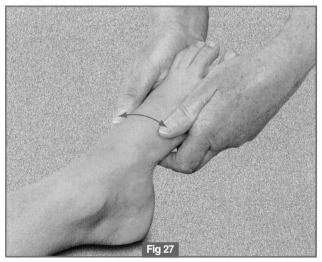

Fig 27

Stretching the receiver's foot.

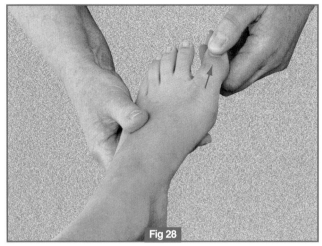

Fig 28

Stretching each toe.

Feet need more pressure applied than other areas which stimulates muscle and nerve endings. If the receiver has ticklish feet, increase your pressure. This will reduce sensitivity. Use firm friction movements over the top of the foot, round the ankle and back to the toes. Then stretch the toes and knead individually. Stretch the foot again, and effleurage the entire leg and foot using long sweeping strokes. Finish with feathering. Each front leg and foot should take 7 minutes to massage.

Through
massage
we realign both mind and body

Back of legs

Turn the receiver face down with the head to one side. Ensure they are comfortable. Placing a rolled-up towel under their feet (fig 29) is also a good idea as it will stop foot cramp. Cramp is a common problem and disrupts massage as well as the receiver's relaxation.

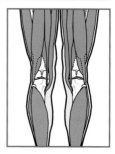

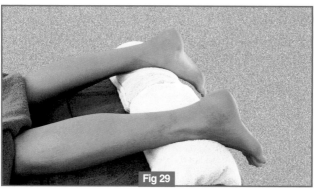

Supporting the ankles to avoid cramp.

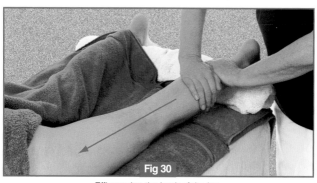

Effleuraging the back of the leg.

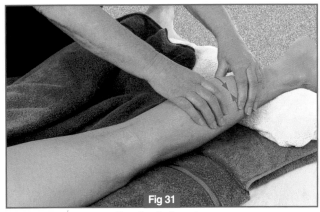

Kneading the lower leg.

Effleurage the length of the leg using long strokes with both hands (fig 30). Start at the foot and finish at the buttocks. Repeat this 6 times to properly warm the legs. Knead the entire leg (fig 31).

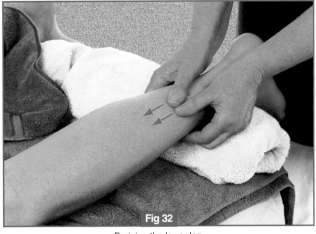

Draining the lower leg.

Draining should then occur (fig 32). Using both thumbs, move from the ankle to the knee, but don't press excessively on the knee as this area is sensitive. Repeat this motion again, sliding your hands gently back to the ankles.

Use the same process to drain the thigh, this time starting at the knee and working into the buttocks. Effleurage the entire leg another 4 to 5 times using both hands and starting at the foot.

Finish by gently feathering (fig 33). Each leg should take approximately 6 minutes for the completed process.

Helpful Hints

- Tell the receiver to turn their head gently from side to side. To avoid stiffness and neck pain which can occur when keeping the neck in one position.
- A back leg massage is effective for tired or aching legs - try one after sport or standing for extended periods.

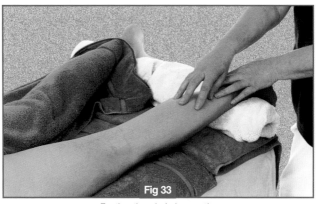

Feather the whole leg gently.

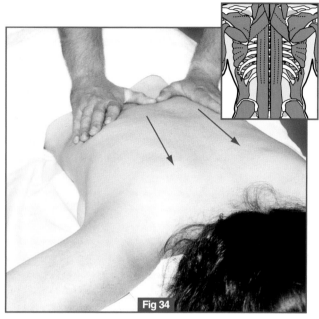

Fig 34

Whilst in this particular massage sequence we are finishing with the back, for many people with aches and pains through back problems it may be more pleasurable to start here. A back massage can make the rest of the massage more relaxing. There is a tendency for all of us to enjoy a back massage to the extent that some may fall asleep.

After applying a reasonable amount of oil, butterfly effleurage the whole back 5 to 6 times. Compression of the back is then carried out with both hands pressing down on either side of the spine (fig 34). As you move from the lower back to the shoulders it will encourage the receiver to release tension which often goes unnoticed. Any remaining tension in the neck or shoulders can be further assisted at this time (fig 35)

The buttocks are also important focal areas for massage - firmly effleurage from the buttocks up the back, releasing pressure as you come back to the buttocks (fig 36). This should be done about 6 times.

Then effleurage one side of the body. Use clockwise friction circles on each side (fig 37), starting at the buttock and going up to the shoulder to help release tension. Repeat this movement three times.

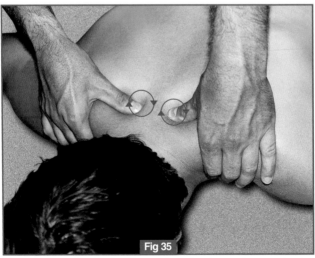

Fig 35

Pressing thumbs into the shoulder muscles make slow rotations covering the entire back of the neck.

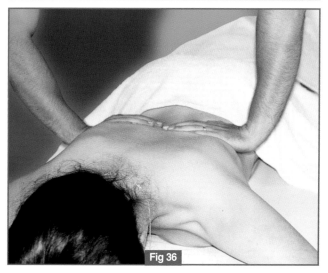

Fig 36

Repeat on the other side. Then, interlacing your hands, use large clockwise circles in the same area (fig 38). Finishing with a gentle butterfly effleurage and feathering. The back massage can take up to 20 minutes.

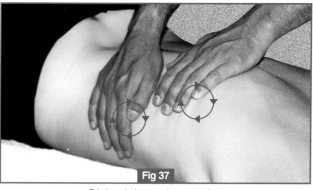

Fig 37

Friction circles to release tension.

Some Tips to Help the Receiver

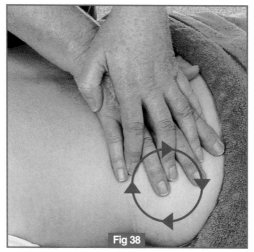

Fig 38

Circling from buttocks to shoulder.

After the Massage

At the conclusion of the massage, remove excess oil with a towel by rubbing downwards from the top of the back to the receiver's ankles (fig 39), making sure no excess oil is on the recipient before re-dressing.

Talcum powder can help remove the oil, but check with the receiver beforehand as some may not appreciate the feel of powder.

Do not hurry a person after a massage - it will often take a few minutes before they are ready to move around. Moving too fast can be an unnecessary jolt to the system.

Loose comfortable clothing should be worn after the massage. Natural fibres are suggested for their breathing qualities.

Massage

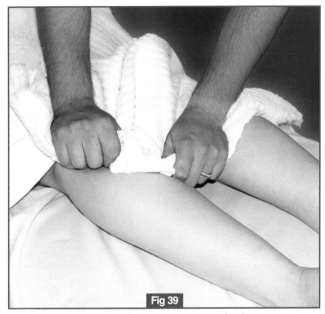

Fig 39

When using oils remember to remove excess after the massage.

Helpful Hints

Where citrus oils have been used, which are photo-toxic,
advise the receiver not to sunbake for 24 hours as the
oils can effect skin pigmentation.

Never give a massage if you are feeling depressed,
anxious or angry. The receiver may 'pick up' on your
feelings and experience unease and even distress.

Massage has not only physiological benefits, but can be
of enormous psychological benefit as it can satisfy the
basic human need for touch and communication.

Aromassage

The power of touch combined with aromatherapy...

For this is the error of our day in the treatment
of the human body, that physicians separate
the soul from the body.
-Plato

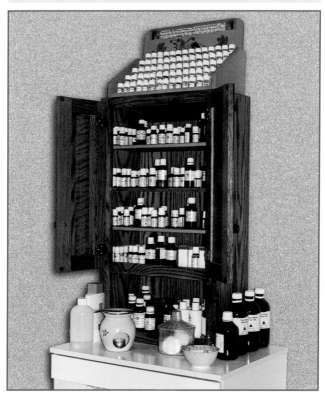

Essential oils are pure plant extracts obtained from various parts of plants, by a method known as slow steam distillation. A pure essential oil is an oil with nothing added or removed, it is whole and pure. The essential oils are obtained from leaves, flowers, fruits, berries, grasses, woods and roots from a wide range of plants grown in various parts of the world and specifically cultivated for distillation.

Essential oils are used in many ways:

- Commercially in the food industry, where distillation methods are used. This type of extraction is particularly rapid, therefore leaving a second or third grade essential oil.

- In the perfume industry - small amounts of high grade essential oils are used along with synthetics, producing both expensive and inexpensive perfumes.

- In Aromatherapy only the top grade pure plant extracts are used, treating the person wholistically, meaning physically, mentally and emotionally.

Pure essential oils have the ability to enter the body's systems through the skin, they are transdermal. However when using an essential oil it is important to know which should be used for a particular part of the body. Please remember more is not necessarily better.

There are oils which I refer to as common oils. These are readily available and bought 'off the shelf'. Following is a list of inexpensive oils which cover many everyday complaints. Commonly referred to as a home first aid kit, added to the massage carrier oil, cream or to the bath, you can inhale them or burn them around the home or workplace.

Caution

Keep essential oils away from children as in concentrated form many oils are toxic.

Massage

Eucalyptus

Radiata non irritant

- ideal for muscle joint pain and for all respiratory complaints.

Contra indications

- Not for use late at night, has a stimulatory effect and can irritate some skins in the bath.

Use for inhalation, burners, massage oil or cream. Suitable for children and adults.

Frankincense Boswellia Carteri

- excellent for mature or aged skins - helps increase a deeper breathing pattern for people with respiratory problems

Lavender Lavandula Augustifolia

- one of the most useful and widely used essential oils. Suitable for all types of skins and age groups. Used to treat minor burns, as an antiseptic for cuts and abrasions, migraine and tension headaches, as a cold compress on the back of the neck and forehead. Very effective for sunburn used in a cream or lotion with some peppermint oil for cooling and soothing the skin. Also acts as an insect repellent, when massaged into the skin regularly in a cream or lotion.

Contra indications

- do not exceed the recommended dosage when using for headaches, an excessive amount will increase the headache. One drop only near the pillow at night will assist and encourage restful sleep.

A typical oil burner

Uses

- massage, bath, burner, heat compress foot/hand baths.
Lemon - Citrus Limonum - can be a skin irritant on sensitive
skins, excellent oil to strengthen the immune system,
combined with Tea Tree essential oil, as a massage rub,
aids in the recovery of glandular fever, flus, colds and
viruses, helps to cleanse and deodourise sick rooms and
other stale areas.

Uses

- massage, burners, creams and lotions.

Contra indications

- do not use in the bath or applied heated to the skin, use with caution on sensitive skins. Lemon is a photo-toxic oil, therefore exposing to the sun 12 hours after application is inadvisable. All citrus oils are photo-toxic and will increase the effects of the sun on skin.

Marjoram Sweet - Origanum Majorana

- an excellent essential oil for muscle cramps and migraine headaches used as a cold compress with lavender. Marjoram is an antispasmodic oil to the muscles and acts as a sedative to the nervous system, works very well on tight tense shoulder and neck muscles; apply within a massage oil.

Contra indications

- do not use a large dosage as it has a sedative action.

Uses

- massage, burners, oils, creams compress aid, bath with other herbal oils, foot baths.

Rosemary - Rosmarinus Officinalis

- an excellent oil for increasing circulation to tired and cold muscles and joints, useful for bathing tired aching feet. Rosemary has the ability to uplift the spirits, improve mental concentration and aid memory. Useful to burn when studying, or encouraging wakefulness.

Contra indications

- can be a mild skin irritant when used in a bath. Do not use at night as it has a stimulatory effect.

Uses
- bath burner massage oils creams foot and hand baths compress.

Sandalwood - Santalum Album
- an excellent skin oil, especially dry mature skins, soothing in a cream for varicose veins, calming for digestive upsets added to a carrier oil and massaged over the abdomen. Acts as a diuretic on the urinary system. Useful for cystitis in a warm compress over kidneys and abdomen. Good for meditation.
Uses
- bath, massage oils, creams, lotions, foot and hand baths, burners.

Tea Tree - Melaleuca Alternifolia
- one of the most useful oils for cuts, bites and any fungal type infections. Can be used neat on cold sores, very good for hysteria, depression and shock. Works to strengthen the immune system for varicose veins used in conjunction with sandalwood in a carrier. Soothes and relaxes tightness and pain. Aids in recovery of cystitis. Use in bath, massage oils, lotions, creams, burner with lemon in sick room, foot baths, fungal infections, warm compresses for cystitis. Can be used for inhalation.
Contra indications
- can be a skin irritant on sensitive skins especially if used in the bath.

Massage

Thyme Common Sweet Thymus Vulgaris

- an excellent safe oil to use over red or white thyme which are major skin irritants. Sweet thyme is safe to use on children and the elderly, helps combat fatigue, is excellent for rheumatism and general aches and pains and the respiratory system, bronchitis, sinusitis, sore throats.

Uses

- bath, massage, oils, creams, lotions, foot and hand baths and as inhalation for respiratory ailments. If using a burner in a children's room remove before sleep. Use an hour before bed time to encourage restful sleep.

Ylang Ylang - Cananga Odorata

- known as flower of flowers. Excellent for the nervous system - anxiety, depression, fear, panic, shock, has the

ability to regulate adrenal flow, calms and slows down the breath and regulates the heartbeat, can help to lower blood pressure, is good for frigidity and impotence.

Contra indication

- heavy exotic aroma can cause headache and nausea if used in a large dosage. Use in bath, burner, massage oils, creams, lotions. Excellent as an inhalant 'on demand' for interviews or other stressful situations, or people with panic disorder to use at the first onset of such an attack.

There are many other essential oils available. Those listed will cover most common everyday complaints. Do not change any medication if you are using essential oils for any of the listed complaints. Essential oils can work with any prescribed medication. Discuss with your doctor if you wish to change your medication.

Essential Oils are powerful and have to be used with care

Adult Dosage
5 drops of essential oil to 10 mls of carrier oil cream or lotion for massage or skin applications.

Bathing: 5 - 7 drops of essential oil in the bath. First run the bath to the correct temperature, then add the essential oils, inhale and relax for approximately 15 minutes. Do not shower afterwards, but simply pat dry and keep warm with suitable clothing so the oils will have more effect.

Safe use of Essential Oils

Burners or Diffusers

Add 3 - 5 drops of essential oils to the water, use a 9 hour smoke-free burning candle. Oils will be transported through the steam into the atmosphere.

Inhalations

Add 3 - 5 drops of essential oil to 400 mls of hot water in a glass or Chinese bowl, with a towel over your head, inhale through mouth and nostrils for approximately 10 minutes.

Foot/Hand Baths

Add 5 drops to warm water or body temperature. Immerse feet/hands into bath and relax for approximately 15 minutes. A foot spa is the ideal way to treat the feet or hands.

Creams and lotions are excellent carriers for oils used on a daily basis. Being non oily and easy to carry in a jar they can be used throughout the day. Five drops of essential oil to 10 mls of cream or lotion would be a safe application.

For elderly, frail or sick people a quarter of the recommended dosage is safe.

2 - 3 drops of essential oil to 10 mls of carrier. Foot and hand baths and bathing should be adjusted to quarter also. Best oils for the elderly - lavender, frankincense and the citrus oils for burners during the day to revitalise and uplift. Elderly prefer hand, arm, leg and foot massage.

Young children from 2 - 12 years should use a similar dosage. Best oils for children - thyme, eucalyptus, tea tree. Mandarin is excellent for hyperactive children in a bath or burner using quarter of adult dose before bedtime.

Infants - half drop - 1 drop for babies to 2 years old. Best oil for wind pain colic - Roman camomile in a sweet almond carrier massaged into abdomen, babies respond very well to touch, massage has a calming rhythmical effect on them.

Conclusion

Pregnancy

There are some precautions with the use of essential oils during pregnancy.

In the first three months as a safety precaution do not use essential oils at all in massage.

After three months various oils can be used in weak dilution. Understandably mothers should be asked to sample the aroma of the oil before application. The olfactory receptors are very sensitive during pregnancy.

It is sensible when using essential oils to check with the receiver for aromas they prefer in nature, for example, woods, fruits, herbs, flowers, roots or grasses, remember the receiver has to wear the oils for at least 4 - 6 hours after application. This will accomplish the most benefit.

When blending oils to create a good aroma, use your sense of smell as a guide. If in doubt simply use one oil or refer to a qualified aromatherapist.

Massage, as stated in the beginning of the book, treats people in mind, body and emotions. But this is not where the benefit of massage ends. Massaging friends, where earlier tensions have occurred, is an ideal way to restore the relationship. Massage can be effective in re-establishing communication channels and relationships.

Hopefully this book has helped you discover the joys of massage and will 'restore radiance' to many people in the future.

Further Reading

The Book Of Baby Massage
Peter Walker (Kensington Childcare)

The Massage Manual
Fiona Harrold (Axiom)

Easy Steps To Massage
Rosalind Widdowson (J G Press)

The Complete Body Massage
Fiona Harrold (Sterling)

The New Guide To Massage
Carole McGilvery and Jim Reed (Sebastian Kelly)

Human Body
(Diamond Books)

A Pictorial Handbook Of Anatomy And Physiology
Dr James Bevan (Universal International)

The Fragrant Art of Aromatherapy
Karen Bailey (Lansdowne)

The Fragrant Pharmacy.
Valerie Ann Worwood

The Journey of a Thousand Miles Begins with a First Step...

the First Steps
series

- First Steps to Meditation
- First Steps to Massage
- First Steps to Tarot
- First Steps to Chi Kung
- First Steps to Dream Power
- First Steps to Yoga

Further titles following shortly:

- First Steps to Reflexology
- First Steps to Feng Shui
- First Steps to Managing Stress
- First Steps to Astrology
- First Steps to Chinese Herbal Medicine
- First Steps to Acupressure

First Steps to...

•AXIOM PUBLISHING
Unit 2, 1 Union Street, Stepney, South Australia, 5069